BASIC BIOGRAPHIES

Charles Schulz

by Cynthia Amoroso and Robert B. Noyed

Wouldn't it be fun to make people laugh every day? That is what Charles Schulz did. He made the **comic strip** *Peanuts*.

Charles Schulz drew the comic strip *Peanuts*.

Charles was born on November 26, 1922. He grew up in the cities of Minneapolis and St. Paul, Minnesota.

This is what Minneapolis looked like when Charles was young.

When Charles was little, he read **cartoons** and comics with his dad. Charles loved to draw, too. He wanted to be a **cartoonist** when he got older.

Charles always loved to draw.

Charles went to high school. Then he spent time in the army. He married and had children. Charles always kept drawing.

Charles lived with his family in California.

Charles drew cartoons of children. His first comic strip was called *Li'l Folks*. It was printed in a Minnesota newspaper.

Charles drew thousands of cartoons.

Li'l Folks made people laugh. Soon more newspapers wanted to show the comic strip.

Charles drew his cartoons at this desk.

Charles gave the comic strip a new name. He called it *Peanuts*.

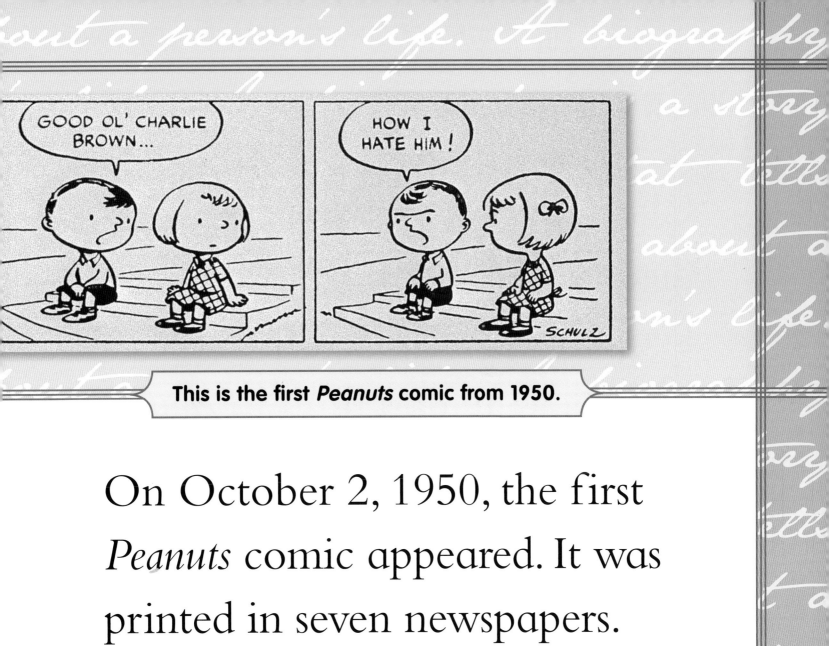

This is the first *Peanuts* comic from 1950.

On October 2, 1950, the first *Peanuts* comic appeared. It was printed in seven newspapers.

Charles drew *Peanuts* until he died on February 12, 2000. People all over the world still love the cute and funny *Peanuts* gang—Charlie Brown, Linus, Lucy, and Snoopy the dog.

Charles, Charlie Brown, Lucy, and Snoopy got an award in 1996.

Peanuts has been made into TV shows, plays, and movies. Snoopy has a giant balloon in a Thanksgiving Day **parade**.

This Thanksgiving Day parade had a Snoopy balloon.

Charles Schulz made many people happy. People will remember him because of *Peanuts*.

Children and grownups everywhere love Snoopy.

Glossary

cartoon (kar-TOON): A cartoon is a funny drawing. Cartoons make people laugh.

cartoonist (kar-TOON-ist): A cartoonist is a person who draws and writes cartoons or comic strips. Charles Schulz was a cartoonist.

comic strip (KOM-ik STRIP): A comic strip is a group of drawings that tells a story. *Peanuts* is a comic strip.

parade (puh-RADE): People marching for a holiday is called a parade. There is a parade on Thanksgiving Day.

To Find Out More

Books

Marvis, Barbara. *Charles Schulz*. Hockessin, DE: Mitchell Lane, 2004.

Schulz, Charles. *Funny Pictures: Cartooning with Charles M. Schulz*. New York: Harpercollins Children's Books, 1996.

Web Sites

Visit our Web site for links about Charles Schulz: *childsworld.com/links*

Note to Parents, Teachers, and Librarians: We routinely verify our Web links to make sure they are safe and active sites. So encourage your readers to check them out!

Index

About the Authors

Cynthia Amoroso has worked as an elementary school teacher and a high school English teacher. Writing children's books is another way for her to share her passion for the written word.

Robert B. Noyed has worked as a newspaper reporter and in the communications department for a Minnesota school district. He enjoys the challenge and accomplishment of writing children's books.

On the cover: Charles Schulz holds a drawing of Snoopy.

Published by The Child's World®
1980 Lookout Drive • Mankato, MN 56003-1705
800-599-READ • www.childsworld.com

ACKNOWLEDGMENTS
The Child's World®: Mary Berendes, Publishing Director
The Design Lab: Design and production
Red Line Editorial: Editorial direction

PHOTO CREDITS: Ben Margot/AP Images, cover; iStockphoto, cover, 1, 8, 22; John Rawsterne/iStockphoto, cover, 1, 6, 22; AP Images, 3, 7, 11, 14, 17; Minnesota Historical Society, 5; Bill Ray/Time & Life Pictures/Getty Images, 9; Bettmann/Corbis, 13; Julie Jacobson/AP Images, 19; Haruyoshi Yamaguchi/Corbis, 21

Printed in the United States of America in Mankato, Minnesota.
November 2009
F11460

LIBRARY OF CONGRESS CATALOGING-IN-PUBLICATION DATA
Amoroso, Cynthia.
  Charles Schulz / by Cynthia Amoroso and Robert B. Noyed.
    p. cm. — (Basic biographies)
  Includes index.
  ISBN 978-1-60253-340-0 (library bound : alk. paper)
  1. Schulz, Charles M. (Charles Monroe), 1922-2000—Juvenile literature.
  2. Cartoonists—United States—Biography—Juvenile literature. I. Noyed, Robert B. II. Title. III. Series.
  PN6727.S3Z62 2010
  741.5092—dc22 [B]
                                                      2009029366